ABDO Publishing Company

BUGS!
Centipedes

Kristin Petrie

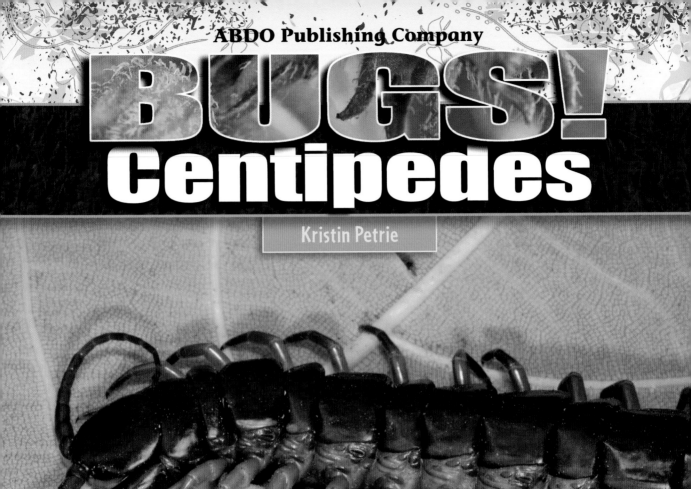

visit us at
www.abdopublishing.com

Published by ABDO Publishing Company, 8000 West 78th Street, Edina, Minnesota 55439.
Copyright © 2009 by Abdo Consulting Group, Inc. International copyrights reserved in all
countries. No part of this book may be reproduced in any form without written permission from the
publisher. The Checkerboard Library™ is a trademark and logo of ABDO Publishing Company.

Printed in the United States.

Cover Photo: iStockphoto
Interior Photos: Alamy pp. 10, 21; Andy Williams/CritterZone.com pp. 7, 15; Animals Animals
    pp. 19, 23; AP Images p. 29; Corbis p. 16; Getty Images pp. 9, 12-13; iStockphoto pp. 1, 17,
    27; National Geographic Image Collection p. 16; Photo Researchers p. 25;
    Wim Acke/CritterZone.com p. 5

Series Coordinator: BreAnn Rumsch
Editors: Megan M. Gunderson, BreAnn Rumsch
Art Direction & Cover Design: Neil Klinepier

Library of Congress Cataloging-in-Publication Data

Petrie, Kristin, 1970-
  Centipedes / Kristin Petrie.
    p. cm. -- (Bugs!)
  Includes index.
  ISBN 978-1-60453-065-0
  1. Centipedes--Juvenile literature. I. Title.

  QL449.5.P48 2008
  595.6'2--dc22

              2008004788

Contents

Slinky Centipedes

What looks like a worm, but has many creepy legs? The centipede! Sometimes called hundred-legged worms, centipedes may be the creepiest bugs around.

Centipedes usually just look like they have 100 legs. In fact, the most common centipedes have about 30 legs. Yet, there are centipedes that live up to their nickname. These long creatures can have far more than 100 legs.

Whether it has 30 tiny legs or 100, a centipede skittering across the floor is an unwelcome sight. To make matters worse, centipedes tend to show up in creepy places. They might surprise you in a dark basement, a damp garage, or a shady backyard.

Keep reading to discover many amazing facts about this creepy, crawly bug. Hopefully by the last page, the hundred-legged worm will seem less frightening. You may even want to get a closer look at this fascinating creature!

Some centipedes are called tiger centipedes because of their striped segments.

What Are They?

Despite a common belief that centipedes are insects, they are not! Rather, centipedes are **arthropods**. A lot of animals are arthropods. These include other creatures with many legs, such as spiders. Yet insects are arthropods, too.

What's the difference between insects and centipedes? Insects are from the **subphylum** Hexapoda. Hexapods have a total of six legs. They also have a total of three body **segments**. Centipedes are from the subphylum Myriapoda. Myriapods have many pairs of legs attached to their numerous trunk segments.

Myriapods are divided into four classes. Centipedes make up the class Chilopoda. Within this class, four orders add up to about 3,000 centipede species.

Each species of centipede has a two-word name called a binomial. A binomial combines the genus with a descriptive name, or epithet. For example, a house centipede's binomial is *Scutigera coleoptrata*.

BUG BYTES

Scientists believe centipedes are distantly related to water-loving arthropods, including lobsters, shrimps, and crayfish.

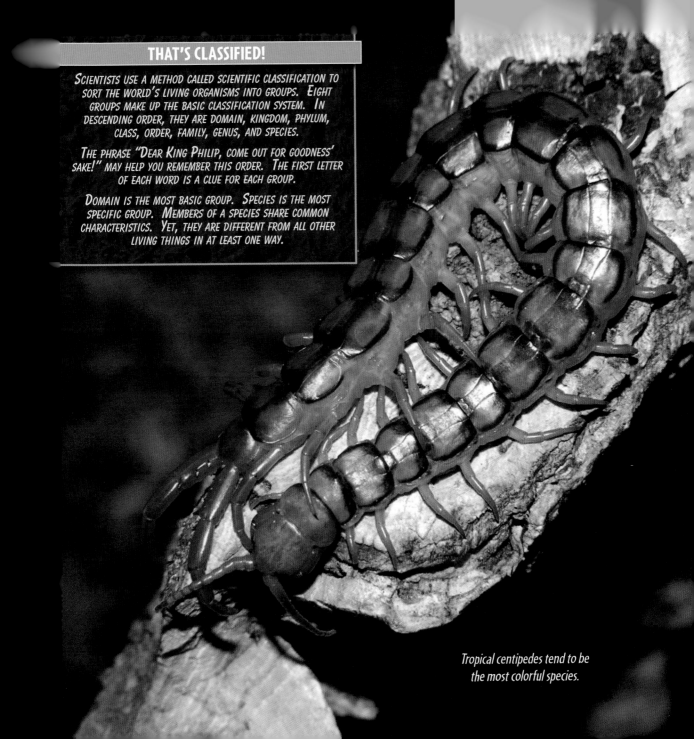

Tropical centipedes tend to be the most colorful species.

Body Parts

The centipede body's two main sections are the head and the trunk. Both sections are covered with a layer of chitin. This hardened substance forms an **external** skeleton called an exoskeleton.

A centipede's exoskeleton determines its body shape. The exoskeleton acts as a frame for the centipede's body. It is a connecting point for muscles. And, it protects the centipede's **organs**.

Centipede bodies are long and narrow with flattened backs. They vary in color from grayish yellow to reddish brown or dark brown. Some larger species have brightly colored markings.

Centipedes also range in size. The smallest are as short as the word *short*. Giant centipedes, the largest species, grow to 12 inches (30 cm) in length!

Chitin covers the centipede's body much like armor. Each segment stacks over the next. This allows the centipede to move its body in many directions while remaining protected.

BUG BYTES

The number of legs centipedes have varies greatly. But, all centipedes have an odd number of leg pairs.

Over time, the centipede's first pair of legs has become a pair of poisonous fangs. This sets it apart from other creatures. In fact, the name Chilopoda comes from Greek words meaning "jaw feet."

The first of the body's two main sections is the centipede's head. The back of the head is fully attached to the trunk. Sometimes, this makes it hard to tell the head of the centipede's body from the rear. The head has a rounded tip and a flattened top. It features the eyes, the antennae, and the mouthparts.

A small number of centipede species have compound eyes. Compound eyes are made of thousands of lenses connected as one. Other centipede species have ocelli. These are simple eyes that detect light and dark, but not images. Most centipede species have no eyes at all. They use other sensory **organs** to gather information from their surroundings.

A centipede's greatest sensory organs are its antennae. Antennae are long and jointed. They often stick out far in front of the centipede. Antennae help the centipede smell food and danger. They also allow the centipede to feel its way around in the dark.

Last on the head are the centipede's mouthparts. The centipede has one pair of upper jaws, or mandibles. It also has two pairs of lower jaws, or maxillae. The mandibles hold food while the strong maxillae crush and chew the centipede's prey.

Behind the centipede's head is its trunk. This section of the centipede's body is made of many small **segments**. They work together as one.

Small centipedes have around 15 segments. Large centipedes can have more than 100! The centipede's trunk segments are nearly identical. One leg extends from either side of each segment.

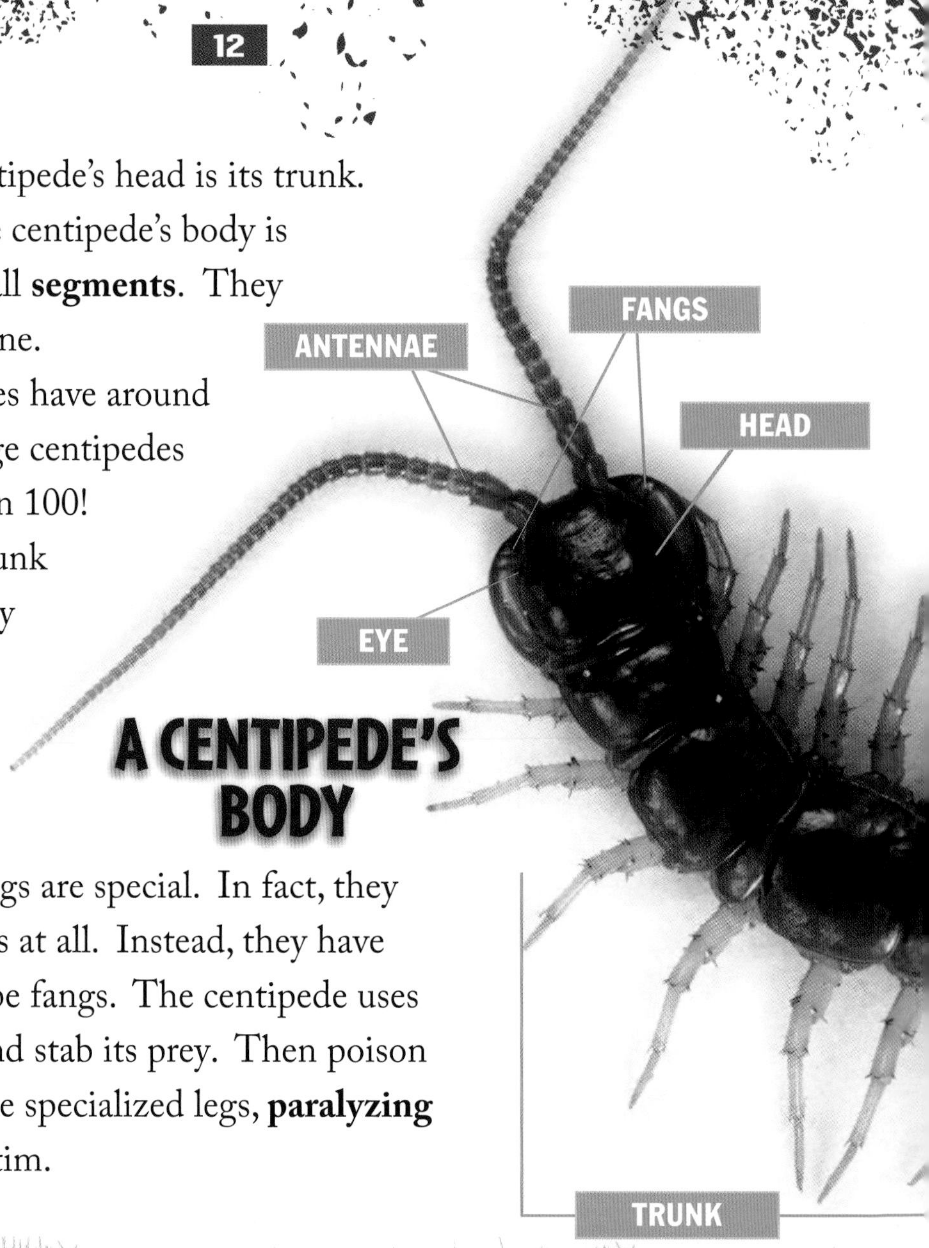

The first two legs are special. In fact, they don't work like legs at all. Instead, they have been modified to be fangs. The centipede uses this pair to grab and stab its prey. Then poison **secretes** from these specialized legs, **paralyzing** and killing the victim.

A CENTIPEDE'S BODY

ANTENNAE

FANGS

HEAD

EYE

TRUNK

Beyond the fangs are many longer, jointed legs. Each leg ends in a small claw. These allow the centipede to move around easily. It can even cling to the walls in your house!

A centipede moves the legs on its left side together and the legs on its right side together. This helps keep its legs from getting tangled.

Like the first pair of legs, the last pair has a special function. In some species, these legs are used for grasping prey. In others, they may function as sensory **organs**.

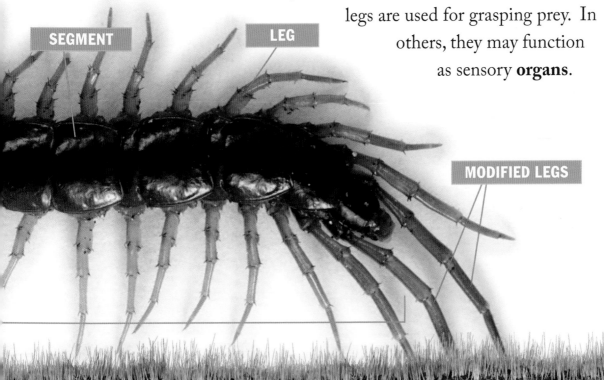

SEGMENT

LEG

MODIFIED LEGS

The Inside Story

Inside a centipede, several systems work together to keep its body moving. The centipede's long trunk houses these important **organs** and body systems.

A centipede's circulatory system is an open system. This means blood flows freely within the centipede's body. This blood is called hemolymph. The heart is a long, tubular organ. It pumps hemolymph from the front of the centipede's body to the back.

The centipede's digestive system has three parts. The first is called the foregut. Here, food is stored or broken down into smaller pieces. The foregut leads to the midgut, where most food is **digested** and absorbed. Following the midgut is the hindgut, where waste is released.

The centipede's respiratory system is made of spiracles and tracheae. Spiracles are holes along the centipede's body. Air enters and leaves through these holes. Tracheae are tubes that connect to the spiracles. They carry oxygen throughout the centipede's body.

House centipedes are the most beneficial species to people. That is because they love to eat other house-dwelling bugs. This might be one reason to keep them around!

Transformation

Centipedes go through a process called incomplete **metamorphosis**. In this type of life cycle, young bugs resemble their parents. They develop gradually into the form of an adult through three stages. These are egg, nymph, and adult.

The centipede's life cycle begins when a male and a female mate. When the female is ready to reproduce, she gathers a web left by the male. The web **fertilizes** the eggs within her body. A centipede

LIFE CYCLE OF A CENTIPEDE

EGG

NYMPH

usually produces 60 or more eggs at one time. Some species produce only one egg at a time. What happens next depends on the centipede species.

Many female centipedes lay their eggs in soil or decayed wood. Some wrap their bodies around the eggs. Others cover their eggs in a sticky substance. These practices protect the eggs from

ADULT

predators. A few species protect their eggs inside their bodies. They give birth to live young.

Eggs hatch to reveal baby centipedes, or nymphs. The nymphs look similar to adult centipedes. However, they are pale in color. Nymphs also have only a few trunk **segments** and legs. This doesn't last long, because the nymphs continue to grow.

A nymph outgrows its skin several times during development. This is called molting. When the nymph is ready to molt, it stops eating and moves to a sheltered area. Next, the exoskeleton splits open at two segments along its back. Finally, the nymph crawls out.

Each molt reveals shiny, soft skin that dries and hardens quickly. The nymph has also grown and added segments. What comes with more segments? Legs! During this time of growth, the nymph goes from a four-legged creature to a many-legged one. The entire molting process occurs seven to ten times before the centipede reaches adulthood.

After about one year, the adult centipede finally emerges. In this stage of its life, the centipede's growth slows down. However, it will continue to molt and add segments and legs throughout its life. The centipede may live five or more years.

BUG BYTES

The house centipede is the only species that can complete its life cycle indoors.

A freshly molted exoskeleton makes a great meal for many centipede species.

Centipede Homes

Centipedes are found in many places around the world. They are common in Australia, Africa, and Central and South America. Warm places in North America, Europe, and Asia are also home to centipedes.

In these regions, centipedes make their homes in various places. These include under rocks and soil and in rotting plants and trees. Sometimes, centipedes make their way into our homes. There, they find damp, cool places to hide out.

You may be wondering why centipedes are always hiding. This is because they don't want to shrivel up! Unlike many other bugs, centipedes do not have a waxy, waterproof coating on their exoskeleton. Without this protective layer, centipedes dry out quickly.

This is why centipedes prefer damp basements, garages, and gardens. There, centipedes can hide in cracks and crevices and under soil and rocks. This keeps them **hydrated** and safe from the hot sun.

Centipedes like tight spaces. Pressing their bodies against another surface closes their spiracles. This prevents them from drying out.

Snack Attack

Centipedes are carnivorous, predatory feeders. This means that centipedes hunt down and eat other live creatures. Their bodies are perfect for this job. They are skinny, bendable, and able to hide in tiny places. When their prey gets near, centipedes attack.

Centipedes are **nocturnal** feeders. Hunting and eating at night gives centipedes several advantages. For instance, sleeping animals are easier to attack than moving ones. Also, centipedes don't need to worry about shriveling up in the cool night air.

A variety of animal foods make up the centipede diet. Ants, flies, moths, and spiders are all favorite foods. Worms and slugs also make a chewy treat for the centipede.

Even small animals are considered lunch to larger centipedes. Mice, frogs, and snakes make tasty meals. Some centipedes even eat other centipedes!

House centipedes love to eat cockroaches and their egg cases. Their great speed helps them catch fast cockroaches.

BUG BYTES

A few centipede species can light up in the dark. Scientists think this may be done to attract prey.

Beware!

Centipedes eat many other animals. However, they are also the favorite food of other natural predators. Birds, mice, snakes, frogs, beetles, and other small animals all feast on centipedes.

How do centipedes protect themselves? These bugs have several self-defense **maneuvers**. The first method is to run away! Their fast legs make this a pretty good escape plan. And their narrow, bendy bodies let them hide in many small spaces.

Amazingly, a centipede can drop a leg when in danger. A dropped leg may distract the predator, allowing the centipede to escape! A centipede can begin to regrow the dropped leg at its next molt.

If these methods fail, the centipede uses its poisonous fangs to fend off an enemy. These sharp fangs dig into the enemy's skin. The poison that follows is often enough to stop the predator for good.

In addition, the claws on every single leg can leave cuts on the enemy's body. Then, poison **secretes** from the centipede's legs into the wounds. This causes itching and stinging.

The centipede is no match for the stabbing claws and powerful jaws of a large praying mantis.

Centipedes and You

Centipedes are common worldwide. Yet, people often mistake centipedes for millipedes. Millipedes are another **arthropod** with many creepy legs. However, they are very different from centipedes.

Millipedes are scavengers that eat dead plants and insects. Unlike centipedes, they will not attack other animals. Millipedes also move much slower than centipedes do. Therefore, millipedes may seem less frightening than centipedes.

Centipedes are mostly an annoyance to humans. No one wants to find a centipede curled up in his or her bed! Yet, people who live in warm, damp regions may often find centipedes in their homes.

Luckily, centipedes are rarely dangerous to humans. They do not carry diseases to us, our pets, or our plants. However, you now know they can attack with their fangs. They can also **secrete** poisonous substances. For this reason, check out centipedes from a distance rather than on your hand!

To tell a centipede from a millipede, count the number of leg pairs on each body segment. Millipedes have two, while centipedes have only one.

You know that centipedes are creepy, crawly bugs. Some people are startled when a centipede appears under an overturned rock or in garden soil. But before that rock or soil was moved, the centipede was doing important work.

The centipede was tunneling its way around in the dirt. This tunneling allows air to enter the dirt and water to be absorbed. Both things make soil richer, which makes plants grow faster and healthier.

Centipedes also eat many of the other pests that bother people, such as cockroaches. And, they eat root-feeding grubs. This helps save many plants from dying.

Some people love centipedes! These creatures prove to be fantastic pets for some brave people. Pet stores and centipede breeders sell giant centipedes. However, centipedes are skilled escape artists. So they must be kept in an aquarium with a tight lid!

The next time you see a many-legged bug, don't squeal with fright. Instead, try counting its legs. Could it be a centipede? You've learned a lot about these creatures. You will now be able to recognize centipedes in the damp, dark places they lurk.

Most centipedes prefer living in the wild. Yet they still enter our homes accidentally. Luckily, giant centipedes cannot sneak around unnoticed for long!

Glossary

arthropod - any of a phylum of invertebrate animals that includes insects, arachnids, and crustaceans. An arthropod has a segmented body, jointed limbs, and an exoskeleton.

digest - to break down food into substances small enough for the body to absorb. The process of digesting is called digestion.

external - of, relating to, or being on the outside.

fertilize - to make fertile. Something that is fertile is capable of growing or developing.

hydrate - to supply with ample water or fluid.

maneuver - a clever or skillful move or action.

metamorphosis - the process of change in the form and habits of some animals during development from an immature stage to an adult stage.

nocturnal - active at night.

organ - a part of an animal or a plant that is composed of several kinds of tissues and that performs a specific function. The heart, liver, gallbladder, and intestines are organs of an animal.

paralyze - to cause a loss of motion or feeling in a part of the body.

secrete - to form and give off.

segment - any of the parts into which a thing is divided or naturally separates.

subphylum - a group of related organisms ranking below a phylum and above a class.